LIFE IN A
ROMAN
VILLA

JANE SHUTER

Heinemann
LIBRARY

First published in Great Britain by Heinemann
Library, Halley Court, Jordan Hill, Oxford
OX2 8EJ, part of Harcourt Education.
Heinemann is a registered trademark of Harcourt
Education Ltd.

Produced for Heinemann Library by
   Bender Richardson White
Editors: Lionel Bender, Nancy Dickmann, Tanvi Rai
Designer and Media Conversion: Ben White and
   Ron Kamen
Illustrations: Bill Donohoe, John James and
   Mark Bergin
Maps: Stefan Chabluk
Picture Researcher: Cathy Stastny and
   Maria Joannou
Production Controller: Kim Richardson and
   Séverine Ribierre

Originated by Ambassador Litho Ltd
Printed in China

ISBN 0 431 113009
09 08 07 06 05
10 9 8 7 6 5 4 3 2 1

British Library Cataloguing in Publication Data
Shuter, Jane
   Life in a Roman villa. - (Picture the past)
   937
A full catalogue record for this book is available
from the British Library.

Acknowledgements:
The publishers would like to thank the following for
permission to reproduce photographs: Ancient
Art and Architecture/G. T. Garvey **17**; Ancient Art
and Architecture/R. Sheridan pp. **6, 9, 10, 11, 12,
16, 19, 20, 25**; John Seely pp. **8, 24, 28**; Trustees
of the British Museum, London pp. **22, 26**
(numbers PS267712, EPS240191b); Werner Forman
Archive/Museo Archeologico Nazionale, Naples,
Italy p. **21**; Werner Forman Archive pp. **23, 30**.

Cover photograph of a Roman villa reproduced
with permission of Rheinisches Landesmuseum,
Trier, Germany.

Every effort has been made to contact copyright
holders of any material reproduced in this book.
Any omissions will be rectified in subsequent
printings if notice is given to the publishers.

Any words appearing in bold, **like this**, are
explained in the Glossary.

 www.heinemann.co.uk/library
Visit our website to find out more information
about **Heinemann Library** books.

To order:
☎ Phone 44 (0) 1865 888066
🖷 Send a fax to 44 (0) 1865 314091
   Visit the Heinemann Bookshop at
💻 www.heinemann.co.uk/library to browse our
   catalogue and order online.

ABOUT THIS BOOK

This book is about daily life in villas
in Roman times. The Romans ruled
from about 753 BC to AD 476. At
first, they just ruled the city of Rome,
in Italy, and the land around it.
However, they formed a strong army
and built a huge **empire** by taking
over more and more land and ruling
it with Roman **laws**. They also
brought Roman ways to the lands
they took over. This included villas –
houses in the countryside, often with
their own farms. There were villas all
over the Roman Empire, from Britain
in the north to Africa in the south.

   We have illustrated this book with
photographs of objects and villas
that have survived from Roman
times. We have also used artists'
ideas of what villas looked like.
These drawings are based on Roman
villas that have been found by
archaeologists.

The author

Jane Shuter is a professional writer and
editor of non-fiction books for children.
She graduated from Lancaster University in
1976 with a BA honours degree and then
earned a teaching qualification. She taught
from 1976 to 1983, changing to editing and
writing when her son was born. She lives in
Oxford with her husband and son.

Contents

The Roman empire

The Romans set up the city of Rome in about 753 BC. By 265 BC they controlled most of Italy. The Roman army built an **empire** of captured lands for Rome. By AD 117 the Roman Empire was enormous.

Wherever the Romans went, they took Roman ways with them. Towns were built in the Roman style. Wealthy, important families, such as those of lawyers and merchants, had villas built away from the towns. They went to their villas to escape busy town life.

Look for these:
The mosaic shows you the subject of each double-page chapter in the book. The picture of an oil lamp shows you boxes with interesting facts, figures and quotes about Roman villas.

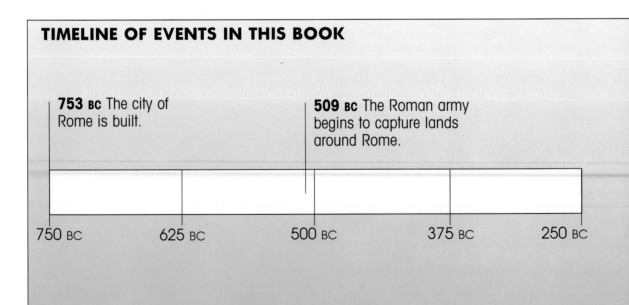

TIMELINE OF EVENTS IN THIS BOOK

753 BC The city of Rome is built.

509 BC The Roman army begins to capture lands around Rome.

| 750 BC | 625 BC | 500 BC | 375 BC | 250 BC |

The Roman Empire
- 265 BC
- 202 BC
- 30 BC
- 117 AD

North Sea

Britain

Atlantic Ocean

Rhine River

Germany

Danube River

ASIA

Gaul

Spain

Rome
Italy

Black Sea

Greece

Mediterranean Sea

AFRICA

Egypt

Nile River

Red Sea

0   500 miles
0   500 kilometres

N

This map shows how the Roman Empire grew until AD 117. It grew too big for the Romans to control. In AD 285 it was split into two parts. But local people began to force the Romans out and the empire ended.

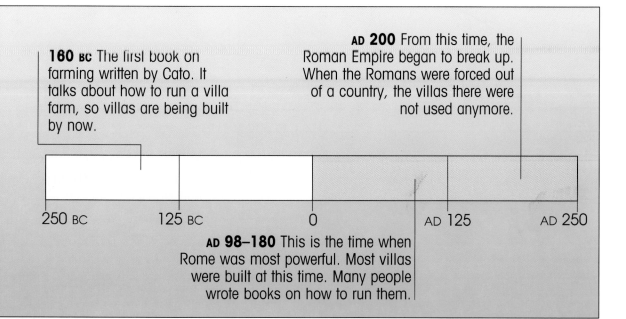

160 BC The first book on farming written by Cato. It talks about how to run a villa farm, so villas are being built by now.

AD 200 From this time, the Roman Empire began to break up. When the Romans were forced out of a country, the villas there were not used anymore.

250 BC   125 BC   0   AD 125   AD 250

AD 98–180 This is the time when Rome was most powerful. Most villas were built at this time. Many people wrote books on how to run them.

Roman villas

Wealthy people lived in towns and used their villa for holidays. Their villas were huge, with orchards, farmland and woodland all around. This made them very private, like country estates today. Less wealthy people lived in their villas all year round. These villas were more like small farms, with a house big enough for the family and a few guests.

VILLA BASICS

Every villa had inside its walls:

- a house for the owner's family
- separate rooms for the slaves and the farm workers
- barns for the animals
- store rooms for the crops and farm equipment
- a **shrine** to pray to the gods.

Villas were built in beautiful places to make the most of the view. Many of them had a **porch**, or shady covered walkway from one part of the villa to another.

Slaves and farm workers lived at the villa all year round. They kept the house clean and well repaired. They looked after the animals and the **crops**. They took spare crops to market and bought pots and pans and other **household** items for the villa. Sometimes there were so many workers that the family hired a **steward** to run things for them.

This is an artist's idea of what the small villa at Chedworth, in Britain, was like. Doors, windows and porches looked out to the countryside or in to an enclosed garden. It had a vegetable garden inside the walls.

The family

Mostly, just the villa owners' family and its workers and **slaves** stayed at the villa. Sometimes the family had guests to stay. These were usually friends, or uncles, aunts and other relatives. The father was head of a Roman **household**. He bought and sold land, **goods** and slaves. He did the shopping and hired workers. He even chose who his children married. Everyone who lived in the villa had to obey him, from the workers to his grown-up children.

Husbands and wives usually came from the same kind of family. This married couple, from a wall painting in a villa in Pompeii, probably came from wealthy families – the kind that would own a villa to go to on holiday.

Roman mothers believed in wrapping babies tightly in cloth bands, as seen on this tomb carving. This was supposed to help their limbs grow straight. It also kept the babies quiet and out of harm's way.

The mother ran the home and looked after the children. She had slaves to help her. Sometimes she taught her young children to read the alphabet, or simple words, or played games with them. Wealthy women without children had slaves to do everything for them while visiting their villa. They sat and admired the view and chatted to the other women staying at the villa. They went for walks or entertained their guests.

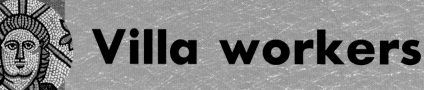

Villa workers

The family needed workers to look after them and run the farm. Most of the workers were **slaves**. Roman slaves were often people from countries captured by Rome. They were bought and sold at markets in the town.

Many slaves were well looked after by their owners, including being paid for special jobs. Sometimes they were given, or allowed to buy, their freedom. They often carried on working for the family for **wages**.

VILLA SLAVES

The most important slaves worked in the house, so spent most time with the family. They cooked, cleaned and looked after their children. Some families had their own tutor to teach the children. Tutors were sometimes slaves, too.

Wealthy women had maids to help them wash and dress. Their maids did their hair, too. Maids had to look after their mistress's clothes and keep all her things neat and tidy. In a small villa, maids also did the cleaning.

Farm workers on villas did all the hard, heavy work. They ploughed the soil – as shown on this **mosaic** – planted and harvested the **crops** and looked after the animals.

Some slaves were well educated, such as doctors and teachers. These slaves were the most expensive to buy. The family had to feed their slaves and give them clothes and a place to sleep. Sometimes it cost less to hire ordinary workers for just when they were needed. These workers were often freed slaves. They did the same work as slaves.

The main house

The family lived in the main house. They wanted it to be as big, beautiful and comfortable as possible. Every house had a main living room, a dining room, a lavatory and several bedrooms. There was no kitchen in the main house. It was in a separate building near by. This was to avoid cooking smells and the danger of fire.

The main house was built to make the most of the views. Seaside villas, like this one near Naples in Italy, had balconies running all along the side of the house that faced the sea.

Bedrooms were the most private rooms in the house. If a house had two floors, the bedrooms were always upstairs. If all the rooms were at ground level, the bedrooms were at the back of the house. This was the part of the house that visitors did not go to unless they were staying at the villa. Bedrooms often opened on to a garden.

HOME LIFE

The main house was comfortable. It usually had:
- a **hypocaust** system to heat some of the house
- a **bath house**
- portable stoves for cold weather
- painted walls
- **mosaic** tile floors.

The dining room was heated using a hypocaust system. Air under the floor was heated from an outside furnace.

hypocaust system

13

The bath house

The Romans believed that keeping clean kept you healthy. They had a quick wash in cold water in the mornings, but spent a lot of time in **bath houses**. Towns had big **public baths**. Most villas were a long way from a town, so the family had their own bath house. This was either at one end of the main house or in a separate building.

NO SOAP

The Romans did not use soap. Instead they oiled their body all over and then scraped off the oil, dirt and sweat with a scraper called a *strigil*. Some families helped each other scrape clean, others were cleaned by **slaves**.

People often took a pot of their favourite oil and their own *strigil* to the baths. They did this even when staying with friends.

furnace

Big villas had a large bath house. This had a steam room, exercise room and even an outdoor swimming pool. The bath house of an ordinary villa often had just a hot bath, a cold bath and an 'oiling room' to oil and scrape in. The whole family, and sometimes guests, used the bath house of a villa at the same time. They sat and gossiped, and even drank and ate snacks.

The bath house had an outdoor furnace to heat the water for the hot bath. The furnace also heated the air to warm the rooms through the **hypocaust** heating system.

The farm

Most villas had some farmland. This land was farmed differently depending on the weather in different parts of the **empire**. In cold, damp places such as Britain, farmers grew wheat and barley for making flour. They kept animals for meat and milk, and used their skins for leather. The owners sold off anything that they did not need, so the farm cost less to run.

This statue of a ploughman shows him dressed for cold, rainy weather. Leather capes, like the one he is wearing, were oiled with animal fat to make them waterproof. It also made them very smelly.

In hotter parts of the empire, for example southern Italy, villa farms grew grapes for wine and olives for oil on steep, dry land. They kept animals such as goats that did not mind steep, bare places. If a villa in these places had flatter land near a river, the farm grew wheat and vegetables.

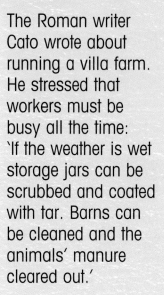

OFTEN BUSY

The Roman writer Cato wrote about running a villa farm. He stressed that workers must be busy all the time: 'If the weather is wet storage jars can be scrubbed and coated with tar. Barns can be cleaned and the animals' manure cleared out.'

Villa owners in hot places often grew grapes to make their own wine. **Slaves** cut the grapes from vines then trod them down to get the juice out, like in this **mosaic**. It was slippery work, so the slaves held on to ropes so as not to fall.

Clothes

Peoples' clothes showed at once if they worked at the villa or were part of the owner's family. Workers wore clothes they could move easily in – loose **tunics** of cheap **undyed** wool or linen cloth. The family wore longer tunics made from expensive cloth, bleached white or coloured, and cloaks to go out in. They usually wore less expensive clothing and jewellery at their villa than in town.

Villa owners wore longer clothes than their workers. Sometimes, female **slaves** were told to wear long tunics, so they did not show their legs. But to do some jobs, they had to tuck up their skirts in order to move freely enough.

Even when they were relaxing at their villas, wealthy women put their hair up in complicated hairstyles. Maids spent a long time helping their mistress dress and do her hair. Working women just pinned their hair up out of the way.

MAKE-UP

Most women wore some make-up. They made their lips and cheeks red with the bits from the bottom of red wine jars. They powdered their face with chalk dust. They darkened their eyelashes and eyebrows with the ashes from the fire mixed up with fat.

Romans wore layers of clothes folded, tucked and fixed with pins or brooches. People slept in a nightshirt and underpants. They put on more layers when they got up. Everyone wore a tunic over their underwear and a cloak when they went out. The villa owners, workers and slaves wore indoor shoes inside the main house, so as not to damage the beautiful floors.

Education

Men and women led different lives in Roman times, so children were brought up to fit these lives. Boys from wealthy families were taught to read, write and speak well. They were also taught to take part in public life and to understand how to run a villa. Lessons did not stop just because the children moved to the family villa. Boys from workers' families learned their fathers' jobs. The sons of **slaves** were also slaves.

This carving shows boys at a school in a town. Sometimes boys had a tutor at the family's villa, but went to a school when the family was living in town.

Girls were taught how to run a home. The daughter of the family learned how to organize the workers. She learned enough reading and writing to keep records. She also learned other skills, such as spinning, that were seen as useful to pass the time. Girls from workers' and slaves' families learned how to do housework, cook and look after the women of the family.

Some girls from wealthy families, like the young woman in this wall painting, wanted more than a basic education. Not all parents thought this was a good thing, but some girls did have tutors who taught them to read and to understand famous writers.

Play

When the boys of the owner's family were at the villa, they spent most of their time playing outside. In towns they played indoors, not in the dirty, dangerous streets. So at the villa they enjoyed racing games, and fishing and swimming in nearby rivers, lakes or the sea. Children of **slaves** and poor workers spent little time playing. They had to start to work from as young as five years old.

Children played with dolls and balls wherever they were. Poor families made dolls for their girls from rags and bits of string, like this one.

HUNTING

Hunting wild animals was an important way for the men of wealthy families to enjoy themselves. Boys went hunting boar, deer and bears with their father and other men staying at the villa.

The children of wealthy families were not allowed to play with the workers' or slaves' children. Girls in these families could not run, climb and chase about as much as their brothers.

Families that were not as rich and important sometimes let all the children who lived and worked at the villa play together. Workers' and slaves' children had to get their work done first.

Men hunted for fun, but it was useful, too. The boys in this **mosaic** have caught a wild boar. Wild boar were dangerous to hunt but made a tasty dinner.

Religion

The Romans believed in many different gods and goddesses who came to Earth and changed peoples' lives. So they spent a lot of time praying and making offerings to the gods, to keep them happy. Towns had **temples**, but there were no temples in the countryside. In the countryside there were **shrines** in special places. People also had shrines in their villas.

NEW GODS

When the Romans took over a country, they often took over their gods too. They just added them to existing Roman gods, so they did not have to stop the local people worshipping them.

This shrine from a villa is to the gods known as *Lares* and *Penates*, who took care of home life. People prayed at the shrine. They also saved some of every meal to burn as an offering, or gift, to these gods.

This carving, from Bath in England, shows the goddess Sulis Minerva. She looks like a man because she is a combination of the Roman goddess Minerva and the British god Sul. She has Sul's face and Minerva's hair.

The family that owned the villa prayed at the shrine in the main house. The workers went to shrines in special places, such as a clearing in a wood, or by the side of roadways. Local gods were more important in the countryside. So were special gods, such as the gods that took care of harvests, animals and of children as they grew up.

Keeping in touch

The government of the Roman **empire** built a network of roads and sea routes across its territory. These routes helped villa owners to get to their villas and send messages there when they were away. Travel was hard, even if a villa was near a well-built road or a seaport. Most villas were less than 50 kilometres (31 miles) from the town their owners lived in. Ordinary people rarely travelled beyond the town.

This letter was sent to Sulpicia, the wife of the man who ran Vindolanda fort. It was written by her friend Claudia, who lived nearby. It invites Sulpicia to Claudia's birthday party.

Wealthy people travelled by road in covered carts pulled by horses. Even with cushions to soften the bumps, wooden wheels on paved roads made an uncomfortable ride. Villa workers took carts to market, or walked with a donkey loaded with things to sell. The villa family travelled long distances by river or sea in boats.

Carts were the most usual way of moving goods between the villa and the nearest market. Sometimes the market was several days' journey away.

Food

The Romans ate three meals a day. Workers and **slaves** ate mostly bread, cheese and vegetables, whenever they had time to eat. The villa owners ate a breakfast of bread and fruit or cheese, at any time from sunrise to 7 a.m. Lunch was bread and leftovers from dinner the night before, eaten at about midday. Dinner was the most important meal of the day. It lasted from about 4 p.m. well into the evening. People ate lots of different dishes, sweet and savoury.

Most cooking was done in pots over an open fire, on a hob like the one shown here. Stews were cooked in pots raised above the fire. Meat was cooked on skewers on the hot coals.

Roman recipe – stuffed dates

The Romans liked to make 'surprise' food. In this sweet, sticky dessert the surprise is that an almond nut replaces the stone in the middle of the date. The date stone and the almond nut are a similar size, shape and colour.

WARNING: Do not cook anything unless there is an adult to help you. Always ask an adult to use a sharp knife or lift a hot tray from the oven.

1 Carefully make a slit in the dates and remove the stones (if not already done).

2 Sprinkle the cinnamon on a small plate. Roll each almond in cinnamon and put one inside each date.

3 Put the dates, cut side down, on a buttered baking tray.

4 Cover each date in a thin layer of honey.

5 Bake at 230 °C (450 °F/gas mark 7) for 10 minutes. Then take the tray out and allow to cool.

29

When the Romans left a country they had taken over, their villas were sometimes destroyed. Occasionally, local people moved into the villa for a while and ran it as the owners did. But soon, local ways of living took over. In Italy, people carried on living in villas as they had always done. Many wealthy Italians still have villas in the country or by the sea, to escape from busy town life.

VILLA RUINS

Archaeologists keep finding villas from Roman times all over countries that were once part of the Roman **Empire**.

Villas, like this one at Pompeii, are the best preserved because they were not excavated until the 1750s. Before this they lay under the ash and mud left by the volcano eruption that destroyed them in AD 79.

Glossary

archaeologist person who uncovers old buildings and burial sites to find out about the past

bath house Roman building with hot and cold baths, as well as a warm room for people to clean themselves in

crops plants grown to provide food or materials, or to sell

empire a country and all the other lands it controls

goods things that are made, bought and sold

household everyone who lives and works in the same house

hypocaust Roman heating system that used hot air under the floor to warm a room

laws rules made by the people who are running the country. People who break these rules are punished.

mosaic picture made up from many different coloured pieces of stone fixed together

porch roofed area to give shelter on the outside wall of a house

public baths town baths that everyone can use

shrine place where Romans came to pray to gods and goddesses and leave them gifts

slaves people who are bought and sold like property. They cannot leave their owners but may be given, or allowed to buy, their freedom.

steward a person who runs a farm or a home for the owners

temple place where people pray to gods and goddesses

trade this can mean:
1 a job, for example making shoes or clothes
2 selling or swapping goods, for instance the Romans traded oil for wheat

tunic T-shirt shaped piece of clothing that comes down to about the knees. Roman men, women and children all wore tunics.

wages money paid to people for doing a job

undyed something that has not been soaked in a coloured dye so that it becomes that colour

More books to read

History of Britain: Roman Villas, Brenda Williams (Heinemann Library, 1997)
People in the Past: Ancient Roman Homes, Brian Williams (Heinemann Library, 2003).
The Life and World of Julius Caesar, Struan Reid (Heinemann Library, 2003)

Index

Titles in the *Picture the Past* series include:

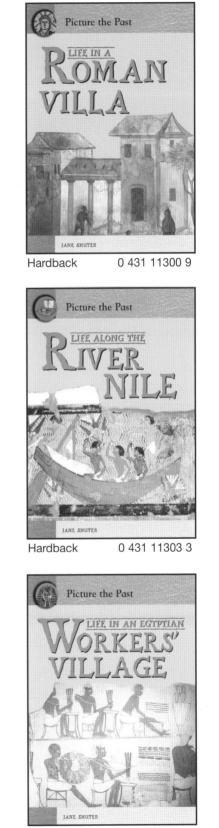

LIFE IN A ROMAN TOWN — JANE SHUTER	**LIFE IN A ROMAN VILLA** — JANE SHUTER
Hardback 0 431 11299 1	Hardback 0 431 11300 9
LIFE IN A ROMAN FORT — JANE SHUTER	**LIFE ALONG THE RIVER NILE** — JANE SHUTER
Hardback 0 431 11298 3	Hardback 0 431 11303 3
LIFE IN AN EGYPTIAN TOWN — JANE SHUTER	**LIFE IN AN EGYPTIAN WORKERS' VILLAGE** — JANE SHUTER
Hardback 0 431 11302 5	Hardback 0 431 11304 1

Find out about the other titles in this series on our website www.heinemann.co.uk/library